Also by czarthepoet

This is True:101

IF THERE WAS EVER

Words for the confidence and love and conviction missing in action within oneself.

czarthepoet

Dedicated to the family I was born with
and the family I was able to discover.
Thank you all.

Foreword.
Forward.

There is a time for love
Time for pain
There is a time for success
Time for failure
But there is always time for growth

If There Was Ever

Star watching
Day watching
When the sun turns
into the moon
I see my mom
only in the day
I see my dad
only in the night
Everything that seems so bright
Everything that seems so night
As cold as the war
too hot too full too empty
nothings ever too dull
Taking time away
to capture every moment
Be you
with the clouds white or gray
Nothing ever stops

Finding the colors
and the corners
and the lines
Finding the quadrants
that kept me blind
Perfect degrees
in every which way
Only thing secluded was me
Being broken manifest the light
the path was naked as I egress

After your first cry
or your first lie
Nothing is quite the same
Let the pain in
it will always help you rise

being peered upon
by strange eyes
familiar emotions
escaping every ounce of pressure
I met every encounter
like the first impression
Not a soul peeped
All eyes could see,
the satisfaction that saturated the room
Bless the decision
Bless the conviction
It could have been anyone
but you paved that road
explicit and distinctive

Fighting like a boxer
Fighting to escape
Fighting like a martyr
Fighting for what's great
Fighting brought me suffering
Fighting to release all this hate
Fighting to contain all that's great
Fighting to put food on the dinner plate

Fight they say
Fight they said
Now I'm fighting to protect
Fighting for what's mine

Fighting to shun all the neglect
Fight for your rights
Fight for the light
Fight for what's right
Go in blind,
Fight with all your heart and might

Putting places into memories
all that you receive
Learn from the negative
leaving positives on the receipts
Pardon me ..
Excuse me ..
When is the search finally complete
It comes down to
zig-zag, ying-yang
Own your own temple
Brace for the light
&don't let it be the end of a gun
Bang . Bang . Bang

Those rich and exposed need to reveal more
show all to be revered
Steer the ship
Band together no matter a consequence
Having us running for sport
Yet dictating the wagon size
Amending the solidity of power
The better the talent
the higher the wall
The escape is there
But they'll pull your card if you fall
Blame it on the problem they gave me

If There Was Ever

Double standards are here
For looks and all to gander
Born from love, taught to hate
draped in elegance
awaiting a grand fate
Simple & rude
But it never came upon me

Breathe out your truth
Realize all the help
Believe in what you preach

I left out some while ago
Stopped the chase
Deciding to retrieve all
the happiness that was
discarded, sorry

How can you love me ..
Only being upset or cordial
What type of being is that

It is all beyond me
No longer can I sleep it off
Nor would I like to forget it
Although living in regret
doesn't seem all too bad

If There Was Ever

Love is sudden
Love is swift
Filled with plenty a twist
Many shifts
As it leaves you cursed
Never gone as it's never lost
Masked pain into pleasure
Possessing all that is your power
Crazed into stealing your composure
Beautiful on every surfaced
But a monster
Born for creation
Love is guidance
Love is grand

Rays of perception come generously
Categorizing any defeat
Championing each victory
No race to compare the experience

Pick up advice
no matter the scene
Not here for a look
Not one document of the rise
Capture the energy
Teach, learn, exemplify

Where did it go
Bump, bruised, tarnished
Recollecting any detail
Every encounter
Evading anything painful
Encompass all to retain true value

Defeat holds no perception
to the possession of greatness
only progression
time is needed to reflect
essential
Constantly surveying landscapes
Sights beyond the realms of imagination

Doing wrong onto perpetual resistance
here to compete within
To learn, then give knowledge
Elevate all that is my world
May it be under control

Feel safe only when we
are alive
Cannot change if you want to
love me
Times has pitted you against everything
about me
Leaving it undecided,
as jaded
Maximizing my patience

Bare skinned
Browned sweeter than sugar
Banned from my treasures
Can this be so simple
Warmed from the moon's light
Blanket as a canvas
No borders or boundaries left
Cut out all the moments
Saturate every wall with presence
Only and ever collage

If I had hands like yours ..
I'd want the world & want it alone

look at what you do to each person you touch .
a reach that goes beyond

ego forging lanes
with my honesty
coping along
feeding gas to the flames
blaming the powers that be

There is no other way
eliminate all the copies

extend my reach
to eclipse all doubts
living in my house of beliefs

Breathing negativity
Exhaled dreams
He was about the people
&how his ways swayed
Believe in yourself before bringing in any strays
There will be times that self-belief
comes from someone else
See everything as wisdom to be gained
Plenty of sources come & go, life included
Seize it all as it appears

If There Was Ever

Plenty of things I want to do
Plenty of things I want to try
Plenty is not what I'm about
Plenty is what I want

Moving towards mastering simplicity
Blessed with what the world can bestow

Too many have false parallels
Expanding their world,
compounding prophets
Confusion between roles tells the real tale

Give me some space
Allow it ..
Creating distance with my pace
Failure in tow

Excellence is the only finish line
Reaching on any glance
How could I give up,
looking at greatness before me

Cracking heads to get the message through
Struggle is not the choice
Depression is not the choice
Image slavery being a choice
Cannot escape the trenches being rooted in the forest
It was known, none of it was fair
Look at us now,
they still don't play fair
History may not be concrete but, tombstones have yet to
be erased

with no limits for ability
bathing in oceans of knowledge
Slipped right on to lust, clearly not aiming for trust
Gained wisdom, love still crept upon my porch
Sweet and innocent
Donating in the form of purpose
to fulfill a destiny
to create in that which is given
Why hide
Why lie
No longer just being
but a conduit

Humans being kind, tentatively
No matter our colors and deformities
our greatness and lack thereof
it all becomes relative
Like the chromosomes constructing all the skin that
curates the youth
cops still trying to press us
Raising oppression and enforcing security
Approaching caution of where I should be
As it happens life is a movie

Put back
Not give back
Set back after set back
Blaze up
Gotta head back to the setup
Blowing past every hinderance

All in and alone
Back to the wall
Climbing out of my place to be
No one will notice

innocence is confiscated
can't even swallow some pride
Pull it back
Obliterate your thirst

Relate only to whom?
Rise before anyone can bring you down
Take all your chances
Shoot every single shot
Set it on sight
Doesn't need to be complex
Need only be yourself

If There Was Ever

Domestically in shades of extreme
Mainly, I could extremely care less
With everyone advising you to say less
Don't be scared to stand up and cause distress
Fill the void between lines
color it in if need be
Don't forget love holds no guidelines
We are supposed to see all the beauty
leaving no shade behind
not lines, nor discrepancies

On a forgiving occasion
stumbling will happen
Lies made of glass
All seems to be half empty
&perpetual motion allows sinister cycles
Then out goes the light
If ever bright, dreams are loaded
Breathing in air that fills the optimist in me
Just as doubt fills me

Struggling along in this land
where the heart is cold
Rain washing up all the sins
&I can't undress before your eyes
Am I alone?
I guess it's all justified
All means by any means

If There Was Ever

Sleep with only your sweetest desires in mind
Looking so far beyond wealth
Climbing the wall, system built, built by me
Reaching beyond the pockets we are tucked in
Now neglecting my rise to focus on my credit score
My dreams complaining
more than my baby mama

Never having the right amount of time
too much or too little
Still learning to share my opinions
holding onto more than just belief
in a place always promoting and provoking
Choosing is to navigate
Being lost may not be the problem
The solstice to photosynthesis
We are too focused on quantifying what we need
to justify the laws of time
The hands of minute and hour jail us in
Realizing the process of progress,
it all becomes infinite

Warm to the touch
Cold through sound waves
a testament to humanity

Hope, wrapped and deep-fried
in the abyss of despair
Covering my emotions
with each pass of the needle
Remedial moves
Staying content
Falsifying happiness

Take the time
read into your own thoughts
Taking munitions into action

Keeping creation,
house your ideals
Grow potential
By way of not being thought-full

If There Was Ever

As a people, we're facing off
They hate more than just your skin
but love everything you place upon the table

What of the culture to build upon ?
Most of us lose before we get to set a foundation
Constantly attempting to cater to society
Collect even the scattered tips

There is much equity with-in-equality
Raising protests in the aim of protest
They're counting stock on the system
We are not striving to rebuild it
Instead, distracted by creating teams and goals
the wall that divides us is immense
too worried about hitting the gym, eating organic foods,
and looking at GIFs

eternally working on giving the word
&feeding lost souls
Don't become busy seeking likes, funneling false hope
Everything does go on
donating to a church only open Sunday
They don't even have hot fudge

If There Was Ever

Before anything else there is growth
You are expecting me to digress
Dip into parts of my past
that drowned before my eyes
No future in that
Everything that happened remains a factor
I'm here for the rise so add more baking soda
Whatever you thought was shared
Left for the rats & snakes
My hand has been bitten once
Twice will never be
Better off forgiving the road that led us here
Head down hands up, praising all the blessings
Remember me as the idea

Allure may be just smoke and mirrors
But I,
the adventurer, the conqueror
Yearns for the quest
Lush and lavish, the fruits that come to bear

Never change plans
just become more unconventional

Ashamed, becoming more fearful
that the glass is half empty
What is there for me to fulfill
As days go by, life continues
dreams fade
Navigating in America
where the American dream is plastered every which way
and forever
All its been about is TRY, TRY, TRY
as long as you're doing, you'll surely get there
Here's hoping my patience will last that long

Drink water, eat right
Make sure your skin is clear
Work your body every other day and sleep right
Push away the bad energy
move at the right vibrations
Detox everything negative in your life

Believe it
Oozing all out your pours
I cannot resist
reaching all your peaks,
mountains and plains

So proud and so scared
Leaving vulnerability with open arms
Hug me long and strong &often
like thunderstorms in the spring
Not sure what my next steps will be

Oh dear what I miss, how I miss
Oh my dear this we cannot escape
Oh dear, oh dear
Everything in this world we possess
Erase the description
Slowly upping the dose
What does it take to overflow
As it stands you are the fountain
Found in everything I see
Oh dear, let's dare
Shape it all before the mold hardens,
as the colors melt
More than artistry
Poetic motions while the music is relayed
Replaying the rotation
Day in, day out

If There Was Ever

Between pops being a soldier and moms being cutthroat
my birth was inevitable
Crafted in a household where emotion takes the backseat
leather belts compiled welts on my skin
Expect me to be bulletproof
my heart inside a treasure chest
Shuffle everything to cause order

My peace lives in chaos
A mind too much on thought
everywhere is where I want to be

Losing myself under a crumbling
gingerbread house
It was all good
Baby crying, baby feeding, baby needs changing
Moved through state lines
Now everything is blurred
struggling to read in between lines
Ripping the apartment to shreds

Claiming my soul has changed
Amazing the fall from grace & unity
walking on streets I've never known
Leaving you with the hope of a right mind
&prosperity, believe it
Hoping you reach all your peaks
Nothing can replace you
I'll apologize for any shortcomings
Please keep being the goddess that you are

Don't expect me to falter
Check the benchmarks

What I consider failures
you consider trophies
Trying to be in the know
giving me extra lives as video games do

growing still trying to reach my peaks
energy breathes deep
If only a scope could see my fears
In a gear that survival is the only goal
Nothing done by my people is unseen
But turned a blind eye
to the shade that doesn't equal mine
No matter the color they don't mind
Pressing down, shining down the light
on what we do elite

If There Was Ever

enough attention
&enough sustenance
everyday
with sun
with water
you grow

All I want to do is cry
&I'm here losing my grip, my grit
Far out of focus
Approaching linear visions
is the fall opulent?
Trying to escape without this feeling

Falling in love with the future
leaves your presents lonely

Running away to escape love
Punishing your body for all sins
Turn in, breathe out

Love is such a learning process
take time, more towards progress
Have you ever known what love is?
Because it doesn't change you
Nor is it the calm before the storm

Leaving our intro awkward, your expectations
never met reality
Sucker to my own pride
Time to upgrade beyond
whatever horizon you see
Don't expect the back seat to be permanent
First, fill in everything you embody
The picture becomes bigger, more vivid
Fear and satisfaction smeared on the canvas
No reason to let life's colors escape you
Imagine every dream in today's shoes
Walking up to each day more comfortable
like the week's end

Open your eyes
Growth with terror can bring great prosperity

If There Was Ever

breathing through current circumstances
where did it all go wrong
or is it all right

giving my thoughts just to you,
neglecting myself

not sure if I have peace
or have become too comfortable in the chaos
cannot be sure of anything
terrible & terrific it is
hiding from every mirror
afraid of meeting my reflection some days
looking at time without understanding the complexion
seeing the world through the people,
glasses full of souls

The next time you see love,
chase it down
Your heart is a terrible thing to waste
From the touches to the feels
Get it and grab it, hold it tight
Letting go may be fatal
Love holds not barring
no boundaries
Connecting all dots in all sorts of lines
Whether it be official, superficial, artificial
This is all love
Built to take on every storm

If There Was Ever

so lost & so found
black holes of parallels
Not sure if I got one
But this is a reality too much of a mirage
Come overnight, a sensation
Left only for storybooks & fairytales

Simulating animations to stimulate brain cells
All this smoke,
suffocating the room
Blessing my thirst
Trying to remember the last time

She's my main thing
Now she's my side thing too
the loves been too good
Admiration comes in many forms but,
mostly flattery

If There Was Ever

Tugging on my neck
Sincerely.
every ounce of your sweat

Spread across my body
Bathe in the essence
Sins of satisfaction

Stop just to start
Jiggle it a little

Night never felt younger
Night never felt more still
Skin never felt so good

Out here trying to gauge
my own morality
through time
lost my own mind
Going over trials
trails & tribulations
stoned. stuck
before truly
opening my eyes

If There Was Ever

Escaping all the treason shading peers & mentors alike
Running for the fences
Love thee before thy neighbor
Forgive yourself to eradicate doubt

Too much is centered around exclusivity
Even I fall in the rabbit hole
Flustered, faulted and ashamed
No longer shall escape be the only exit
Trying to resolve the obstacles braided in my psyche

Attempting to step out of all realms
that is my zodiac sign

There is nothing beyond the reach
More is all my eyes can see

Too many expectations raising me
higher than a soapbox

Learned how to love&hate
Learned of love&hate
It's all about you&I
All the positives&negatives
Anything that is us&we
Simple as hot&cold
The consistency of fucking&fighting
Stronger than thunder&lightning

Creation is time
blossom ideas in the waiting room, have patience
Never knew a hand,
that would block my son

I miss them all
every ounce of blood I can't see on demand
I miss them all

tia, you bathed me
Loved me
Missed those last few years, before you left us
But you have taught me to keep in touch
to reach out more
Family is bonded by more than blood
It's the memories
My home away from home
You are resting now looking down upon your family

If There Was Ever

Never really been into obsession, in return, passion has
always been out of arms reach
might just be an out of convenience type of nigga
But I ain't easy
Hardly ever try to take it easy
No regrets and that's where my happiness comes
shocked of the emotion, I lack
Maybe my soul is too old
My parents were too great, too tough
Gave me a life without fight
Conquer that in which my dreams bait me
Spirit chaotic & murderous
Searching for the monk in me
&no not because I'm bald
fixing to gravitate towards ascension
Being grounded to my roots

Too many timid thoughts
Too many lonely walks
Knowing all too well
connections fade

Wasting my life away
Can't put this knife away
Whether it be goodnight or good day
Shine for everything that doesn't go my way

Learning about this relationship with myself, I can't
believe where I was all this time. Pulled to every edge of
the compass trying to channel the future and the past.

If There Was Ever

felt like our souls touched
We laid in Eden's garden
And I tied you to the trees like bed posts
with each cadence and syllable creating waves
I'm drowning in your devotion
No ice on self-inflicted wounds
Kisses make the pain go away

Now I'm struggling as I condemned myself
&you expect only me to save us
But my homebody moves to the sounds of nature
Just listen to me
Believe in me
All things lead to spreading the sea &we ran together
where does it leave us

Realize what you have before it becomes complicated
Now I'm stuck rolling with anger in the passenger
Ready to bust off at the mouth
Hands filled with clips
No safety in eye's sight
What of an emergency
Diving into surgery
Purge the hatred within me
Voice is filled with glass, cracking and cutting
But you can't see the fear in my eyes
Feel the pain in my heart
I'm sorry

Don't know how much I could hang on
How much I could put us through
Sorry for all the bullshit I put you through
Sorry I can't express to you
all that plagues my mind, my soul

Time is where the devil followed me
God couldn't find me
in Eden and the fruit was overbearing
The weight of things seen
can never measure up to my dreams
So, the love will be mine
The pleasure is all mine

If There Was Ever

my parents being so far gone for so long
This is the time in life I'm waiting for life advice
Took so long to age
so far from reach
so far from the cold
But this
Tilted off-center
this is my journey

Need more life to me
More light to see me
Going to get back to me
Get to all the love that left me

Working on the great escape ..
To blankets of sand, sun rays and living out quotes of my
favorite songs
Just love me
don't judge me
When has man been kind
We have infectious tendencies
cursing any not marching to the wave
What are you willing to live for?

Still in search for the perfect recipe
Living a broken life
You know the working class,
working for sore backs, foot aches, and no brakes
Found a profession that fills my heart
&lines my pockets with lint
Stacking hustles, losing sleep
to bring my ends anything to eat

If There Was Ever

Do not conceive that I am scared to take blame
Listen, it's all on me
Tripping attempting to give you the original
Not too sure if something is broken inside of me
cancer flooding our airwaves
&all this motion is my sickness
Why do we need to stay on this ride
Cancel the flight, please!

Plead my case for stupidity
Defining loyalty changed as we progressed
Kept more to myself
Dedication never faltered
How could you think it would not be you and I
Bask in that essence
The past was part of depression
You gave me insight into a future
Dedicated to investing my gold coins
now we don't share
now we don't care
Delusional, thinking nails and glue will get us back

Deflecting any gaze
Sinking into despair
Delicate with the recovery
Any fares to pay will be my demise

Lost her
I'm losing it
Lost them
Lost our we
Take me back
Show me love
Again Again & Again

I don't know
But I remember

Still
Think of you
Lay with you
Lost without you

We lost it
I gave up
Did less
&did the most
Sorrys can't ..
Don't measure up

If There Was Ever

Never be happy sitting idle
Creativity can die
Just imagine how many levels are left to go
Dabbling in the basics every night

Do it for free
Do it for fun
Do it for love
Do what you do
Bless it upon the earth

Those finding hate
cause & affect growth
you're feeding off recycled emotions
Keep bringing that same energy
Jealousy and envy are congratulated on their lack of
information

having medicine, yet you still choose death
It is all a part of you, I guess
just as sugar to sweetness
oxygen to breath
so proud and so scared
no matter how deep the scar
always recover

If There Was Ever

Reaching beyond just to stretch my capabilities
Aiming to become more complete
Here in America where we compete
Some must fight
Whether it be health, poverty or bigotry

Looking for answers
no doors have opened yet
No reason to stop trying keys

make sense of it all
It becomes common
more relative
Don't wait on any congratulations
They just want to see you broken
gather up all the pieces
keep your dedication
At one point it will all click

If There Was Ever

I'm dumb enough to never be wrong
a know it all
but I do love myself
I would be remised without my arrogance
Senses all displaced
How would I grow without my ego?
who else will believe in me
if I ever let go

Left it up to chance
when I should have given it purpose
I could have accepted the consequences
At his moment I am barren
Never thought it would come to this
I will be lost until I can find you again

Painting pictures, making memories into history
Living beyond societies means
Double standards are still high in all regards
Climbing to elevate the state of mind
Learning more about the negatives,
preaching positivity
Attracted to violence, more than money can deliver
Open your eyes
We gave them the DNA
passed the blueprint
What else should we expect
What else should we accept
Any sign of an up rise would come as a surprise
Heads aren't held high
only being slapped with compromise

The shadows fight back the light as the room dims. The air is sweet, fill with the proclamation of spring. I stand before you as if Eden was our home. You like your wrists bound tighter than a virgin's lips. Eyes wide, legs even wider than the seas. My tongue creeps up from your heels to your knees. I'll raise my head up just as the sun rises, split your pink lips with a simple kiss.

There is something no one can take away
Just realize all you possess
Walking around looking for power
rather than lead
Instead, let your heart empower
choices will become clearer

Paint me happiness
Every shade
Stroke by stroke
Enjoy the process
Become satisfied with progress
Proceed to inspire

If There Was Ever

I need love
I need lust
I need pain
I need hope
I need to suffer
I need to feel

I am typical
I am old fashioned
I am stubborn
I am sane
I am skeptical

I need who I am

Timeframes lose focus
Had a taste of life's bitterness
trying to set expectations
beyond your perception
Time is the only currency
currently counting

I want to apologize to myself
I want to apologize for not doing as much
What I haven't decided to achieve
Where I have let things go

It is understood that you will not attempt to understand
The republic has turned into publicity
In which it fails to stand
Constructed and dismantled all in a day
Being said that the land was free and the homes brave
They have a shield that they're supposed to symbolize
But they hide behind that shield
when the bullets become lies
supposed to be our shield from anything that puts us down
any chance they get we are ostracized
it's impossible to break what has been created to be broken

If There Was Ever

my eyes, now clear before the clouds pass
Viewing everything through the future to the past
Managed to amass a gift elevating me in search of any
stars in arms reach
But in the night
I see so much black on black crime that it breaks daylight
No headway on the horizon
We are no longer broke and bare
just fighting over which shade of the same color
reigns supreme

What would change if we were reading a sentence instead
of counting how many years to complete one? Shot in the
back, choked in the streets, ran out the bleachers. They
come for us even in our sheets. Learn from the dope boys,
the scholars, the slaves. Trying to be those in charge and
cannot take an order. How are you expecting to take the
reins?